MW01706202

Patchwork of the Soul

Patchwork of the Soul
A Quilt of Healing and Wholeness

Jennifer Gaye, M.Ed. & Melissa Haggins, OTR/L

Sister Scribes Publishing
Atlanta Chicago

On the front cover is a photograph of the quilt that the authors made during the writing of this book.
Cover Photos: Curtis L. Gaye

ISBN 09767777-0-3

First Edition, March 2005

Sister Scribes Publishing

Atlanta, GA 30316

Dedication

To all of the women who have gone before—

Inez

Oneida

Gladys and

Candice Bea

Mama Carrie

Precious

Lucy Bell and

Ella Lee

Safronia

Mabel

And of course

Barbara....

Because of you

We ARE.

Acknowledgements

The authors would like to thank the following for their support throughout this process: our parents, our friend and attorney Kenneth Woodberry, Patricia Broat and Karen Casey. Additional thanks to Hancock Fabrics' employees at the North Broadway and North Riverside Mall stores in Chicago and the North Decatur Road location in Decatur, Georgia.

Thank you God for the gift of two lives in one lifetime. With deepest gratitude to the Narcotics Anonymous® fellowship: your love covers me like a warm quilt on a cold night. Thank you to Joyce, Faye, Joanne, Hope and Leslie for your unconditional love and spiritual guidance. To Dr. Euseni Perkins, for believing in me from the moment you met me. Beverly, thank you for your tough love. Ray thanks for the lessons. I would also like to thank Dr. Myra Jackson and Letha Mosley for your inspiration and support through college. To Mrs. Harris a.k.a. "momma" and Kela—thank you for believing in me. To the women in my "inner healing circle"—I love you.

MH

I thank the universe for the gift of creativity...
To JAW and SBH—thanks for being the "friends I can call at 4 a.m."

JG

Table of Contents

"Healing does not represent the closure of the needs of the heart; rather, it is the doorway toward opening your heart."

Carolyn Myss

Foreword

By Barbara Gaye

I HAVE A PASSION.

My passion is to have the best possible relationship with each of my two daughters. It has been a journey getting to this point. My daughters, Melissa and Jennifer are eleven years apart in age and for most of their teenage and adult years they were estranged from each other.

Since I am an only child, I have always wondered what it would be like to have a sister to talk to and share secrets with, to have a shoulder to cry on and just to be there for whatever the situation. After becoming mother to two daughters, I was sure their relationship would be great. Jennifer would have a big sister who would be there for her no matter what and Melissa would have someone to "look out for."

However, due to life changing and life threatening events in both their lives, a sisterly relationship was non-existent. Melissa went through many years of "active addiction" before she finally decided that enough was enough. She went back to school and eventually graduated from The Medical College of Georgia as an Occupational Therapist. My second daughter, Jennifer, evidently suffered from depression and it became very difficult to have a relationship with her. After years of emotional distress, she made it through college and eventually earned a Master's Degree from Georgia State University and is now a teacher. In 2003, she was diagnosed with cancer. She endured all that comes with the disease: radiation, chemotherapy, hospitalizations, medications and mental torture but her treatment and surgery proved to be successful and she is now well.

As a mother, the devastation of seeing one daughter destroying her life with drugs and of my not knowing if she was alive or not and then having the other diagnosed with cancer is unreal. I have cried so much over the years that sometimes I feel I have no tears left to shed. But what a much stronger woman I am today because then I could not do anything to change what was happening to them. It was only when I finally turned everything over to God and left them at the altar that I began to feel some of the burden lift.

During the past few years I have witnessed the slow healing and bonding process between them and as a result of their coming together this insightful, wonderful and touching book was born. When the two of them came to me with the idea of this book and quilt, what I was witnessing was nothing less than a miracle. In the end, when I am no longer here, they will have each other and what a blessing that will be!

Introduction

The experience of writing this book has been interesting to say the least. It all emerged out of my sister's years of ceaseless networking and persistent phone calling. In those years, she would call me as well, sometimes sounding a little frustrated but usually, sounding excited about some synchronistic connection she'd made or some opportunity she'd been given that would get her closer to her goal of opening a facility which would provide supportive services for ex-offenders with substance abuse problems. She always included me in her plans, talking about all of the great ways that my talents and skills could be utilized. Her ideas sounded appealing because I was the kind of person who believed that if I had to work, I should do something that I enjoyed and at which I was naturally good or I should do something that made a difference in someone's life or in the world.

We began to put together a few small proposals and she began submitting them to various people. Time passed, I was diagnosed with cancer and began another phase of personal growth.

During this time, I talked to her about letting go of the "need to please" and what it meant to love your self enough to set boundaries and value on your time and energy. In our conversations, we often hit on common themes in our personal healing journeys. We began to realize that, though our life paths had been different, our lessons had been fairly similar. Furthermore, we understood that our story was unique in that we were sisters whose relationship had also undergone its own healing. We realized that others might benefit from the lessons we've learned. These lessons are not new-just newly phrased. Sometimes, this is what the human mind needs: a new version of timeless truths.

Jennifer Gaye

January 29, 2005

Atlanta

As I drove to Starbucks during my lunch break that Saturday in November of 2004, I called my sister to discuss our strategy for completing "the book." During the past couple of weeks, I had spoken with Patricia Broat, coordinator of the Hazelden Foundation's "Women Healing"® conference and we were meeting with them in December to discuss the proposal we had submitted earlier that year. During my lunchtime conversation with my sister, I said, "You know we will have to have the book finished soon because I feel in my Spirit that we will be chosen as presenters for the "Women Healing" conference, and we have to be published." She replied, "I believe we will be selected as well." That conversation was the beginning of this book. I had, over the years, written my own story to be published at the "right time." I never dreamed I would be co-authoring a book with my sister-especially not about our life journeys! Only in recent years have we formed a relationship where we shared some of our most intimate feelings with each other. Only in recent years have we grown to a point with each other where we have been able to share honestly what it has been like with and without each other. I always dreamed of being the "big sister" I felt I had never been for her. Estranged for many years, our paths had been similar, although divergent.

In a matter of lunchtime, we made the decision to make writing and sharing our "healing stories" a priority and a reality. I am living the life I have imagined! Now I have my sister to share it with!

Melissa Haggins

February 14, 2005

Chicago

PART I.
BEGINNINGS

Chapter 1

A Brief History of Quilting

> The same type of handiwork that has sheltered the simple peasant from wintry blasts has adorned the great halls of doughty warriors and noble kings. Humble maids, austere nuns, grand dames, and stately queens all have shared in the fascination of the quilter's art. And all have contributed to its advancement. Cottage, convent, and castle, all have been enriched by the splendors of quilting and the pleasures of its making.[1]

Quilting occupies an important place in the social and cultural history of humanity. The history of quilting is woven throughout the histories of a variety of different ethnic and racial groups across a long span of time. Though quilting developed out of necessity, it evolved into an art form. Along the evolutionary path of the quilt, numerous techniques developed and were perfected. It is not within the scope of this book to detail all of the various technical nuances of quilting. There are several

---

[1]"A Collection of Notes on the Historical Aspects of Quilting" www.katerynde develyn.org/quilting

great books on the subject and the reader can find a few listed in the resources section in Appendix B.

Instead a brief cultural history of quilting will be featured here, acquainting the reader with the "highlights" of this practical art form.

Quilting and the Ancient Egyptians

Though quilting is traditionally thought of as a fairly recent, "western" art form, there is evidence to suggest that ancient civilizations used quilting techniques. Archaeological finds have revealed carved ivory statues that suggest that the ancient Egyptians may have used quilted material as articles of clothing[2] and the earliest quilted artifact in existence is a ceremonial canopy used by Egyptian queens that dates from around 980 B.C.[3] Even though this quilt is made of pieces of dyed leather rather than pieces of fabric as most people typically associate with a quilt, it does demonstrate the technique of "piecing together" many elements in an artistic arrangement to be used as a cover or decorative item.

Quilting in the Ancient Far East

---

[2] A Collection of Notes on the Historical Aspects of Quilting" www.katerynde develyn.org/quilting

[3] Ibid.

Quilted artifacts have also been found at many archaeological sites that seek to unearth the mysteries of the ancient "Far East." Artifacts exist from the earliest cultures of Japan and China and particularly fine examples of quilting have been found at sites of the nomadic tribes of Eastern Europe in what is now Russia and Siberia.[4]

Quilting in Europe: The Middle Ages and Beyond

When we think of Europe during the middle Ages, many of us get images of drafty castles laden with woven tapestries to keep out the cold. But quilts were also used in a similar fashion. Churches and castles alike employed large quilts as re-enforcement against the elements. Quilted coverings were hung in doorways, sometimes on the inside of the door as an additional buffer and sometimes alone as a substitute for the door itself.[5]

Knights during this era used a quilted vest of sorts underneath their chain mail. The vest served

---

[4] A Collection of Notes on the Historical Aspects of Quilting" www.kateryndedevelyn.org/quilting

[5] Ibid.

not only to keep them warm but also to offer some protection against arrows in battle. [6]

By the 1800s quilted articles of clothing became popular with women wearing thick, quilted petticoats and men wearing waistcoats of a similar style.[7]

Quilting during the Victorian Era

This is era of "quilting bees" and the time period that Americans most associate with the tradition of quilting. The concept of quilted bedcovers had already developed in Europe prior to the seventeenth century and by the eighteenth century quilts were beginning to be made in America as well. By the Victorian era in the late nineteenth century, quilting was a regular part of domestic life in America and Europe.[8]

Quilts from this time period began to take on distinct differences according to regional, ethnic or religious sensibilities. Certain "classic" or "standard" patterns emerged: "log cabin" "wedding ring" and "tulips" are among the more popularized patterns.

---

[6] Ibid.

[7] A Collection of Notes on the Historical Aspects of Quilting" www.katerynedevelyn.org/quilting

[8] Gordon, Maggie McCormick, *The Quilter's Resource Book,* Chrysalis: London 2004

Quilts would also have a great deal of embroidered embellishments, perhaps verses of biblical scripture or the names and histories of family members. Quilts during this era became more "planned" in that even though quilts were still serving a practical purpose, quilt makers began to employ more aesthetic sensibilities.

Slavery and Southern Quilting

Technically, the fundamentals of "Southern Quilting" and that of "Slave Quilting" are very similar. Most of what we have in terms of artifacts and history from the eighteenth and nineteenth centuries suggest that American quilts were mostly patchwork. Some told stories— others recorded familial or community events and dates while still others focused on developing more complex techniques for quilting stitches.

However, quilts made by slaves often contained hidden messages for slaves who were trying to reach free states. During the period of slavery, an escape route known as the "Underground Railroad" developed. This route was made up of men and women who helped slaves that wanted to escape. These men and women would provide food and shelter for slaves on route from southern "slave" states to northern "free" states.

Quilts were used as navigational tools. Without arousing much suspicion, a quilt could be hung on a clothesline or tree as if to dry or to air. The design of the quilt would have been done in such a way as to point out the path of safety to the escaping slaves. The quilt might have the pattern of the North Star or of "arrows" disguised in a pattern of strips to assist the slaves in their journey to freedom.[9]

Contemporary Quilting

These days, quilting has truly evolved into an art form. With the emergence of computers, quilts have been able to become more detailed and quilt makers have begun to incorporate scanned photographic elements as well as intricate computer generated details into modern quilting. While appliqué and traditional patch working techniques still have their place in quilting, technology has helped to expand the artistic playground.

Quilting as a Metaphor for Healing

An overarching theme in the history and tradition of quilting is that of "piecing together" different elements to make something "whole." In

---

[9] Dobard, Raymond G. and Jacqueline L. Tobin *Hidden in Plain View: A Secret Story of Quilts and the Underground Railroad.* 2000

quilting different pieces of material are sewn together to form a whole pattern or overall design. Additionally, the relationship between the parts and the whole is interdependent. All of the parts are needed to create the whole, yet alone the parts do not show the "big picture."

The same can be said of healing. There are many different elements involved in healing. People go through an individualized process but there are a few principles that are extremely important for the healing journey: *love, forgiveness, hope, trust, community, solitude, patience and personal responsibility*. We must engage with all of these principles if we are to truly begin what will be an ongoing process of healing. Remember that healing is rarely ever a spontaneous occurrence and so we must allow the time for this process to occur.

Chapter 2

Our Stories

"Mistakes are part of the dues one pays for a full life"

Sophia Loren

Jennifer's

I suffered from depression for many years. In fact, for many years, the feelings of hopelessness and pointlessness were such an integral part of my daily existence that I began to think that it was the normal way for me to live. I don't quite remember when this sense of hopelessness engulfed me but it had to have been around the time that I was a freshman in college. I had been an excellent student in high school—good grades, accolades, praise and all that. I was certain that the world was waiting for me with open arms, ready to offer me whatever I asked. After all, everything in my life up to that point had come relatively easily for me. There was no reason for me to suspect that college and beyond wouldn't be just as easy. Needless to say, life doesn't always go according to our plans.

When I graduated from college, I wasn't sure of what I wanted to do. I'd decided against my original plans of going to graduate school to become a college English professor. Something in me had changed during my four years in college and I no longer wanted to sit around writing books about books. Though I enjoyed literature—talking about it, writing about it and all, I no longer wanted to make my livelihood at this. It seemed silly to me to sit around analyzing books for a living when there were real problems in the world that needed to be solved. At the very least, I felt that I would be better off learning a trade than becoming a college professor.

While I explored different jobs and "tried to find myself," I spent a great deal of time neglecting my body and my health. There was a period when I didn't get regular medical examinations because I truly didn't care enough about myself to do so. Eventually all of my behaviors—emotional, mental and physical began wrecking havoc on my body and manifested in cancer. I was fortunate and found a wonderful doctor who loved me and encouraged me to "act like a well person not a sick one." Even though I am a "survivor" of cancer, I don't refer to myself as such. To do so would mean to wear my illness like a badge or to immerse myself in what

Carolyn Myss has termed "woundology" in her book *Why People Don't Heal and How They Can.* She writes:

> We are not meant to stay wounded. We are supposed to move through our tragedies and challenges and to help each other move through the many painful episodes of our lives. By remaining stuck in the power of our wounds, we block our own transformation. We overlook the greater gifts inherent in our wounds–the strength to overcome them and the lessons that we are meant to receive through them. Wounds are the means through which we enter the hearts of other people. They are meant to teach us to become compassionate and wise.[10]

Like Myss suggests, I viewed that time period as a great learning experience for me rather than a period of great suffering. Undoubtedly, it was a period of deep sadness for me. I faced many issues during that time and one of the most prominent things that I had to look at was my own mortality. Having a major illness is the ultimate in "baseball bat spirituality." Some higher power is trying to get

---

[10] Myss, Carolyn, *Why People Don't Heal and How They Can,* Three Rivers Press: New York, 1997

your attention and teach you a lesson about some aspect of yourself. Probably, this higher power has been sending you clues and signs and messages for a long time to try to get you to awaken. Certainly this was the case for me. There had been signals along the way. I had ignored many feelings emanating from my gut, disregarded more than one red flag. But I have discovered that our spirit is very persistent. It will try to capture your attention in one way or another. Whether or not you choose to focus your attention on the lessons being presented is, of course, up to you. I've also found that the more we ignore the signals and red flags, the more dramatic the signals and red flags become. Eventually, if we ignore the signals long enough, spirit will send some large, life-changing event to our lives to really shake us up. It is as though the universe is using a baseball bat to hit us over the head and is saying, "Okay, look at your issues and change some things or suffer severely." Dealing with cancer was this type of life changing event for me. Spirit was saying to me in very clear terms "Look at your issues and change some things or *die."* I chose to take heed.

Most people have this kind of moment in their lives—a moment or series of moments that is so dark that you believe you will never be able to see light again. This is the "rock bottom" experience to which some people refer. However, everyone does not always heed the lessons of the spirit, even when they have reached their personal rock bottom. Change is uncomfortable and for many people, it is easier to remain in the habitual misery of our lives. Michael Levin said "Sometimes we stay in hell a long time because we have learned the names of the streets."

The lessons I learned because of my illness are multiple and varied. But the big one that I realized—that *I internalized and decided to start living by* is that ***life is too short to try to please other people.*** My healing did not truly begin until I stopped trying to make everyone else happy and started listening to and honoring my own needs. Once I did that, I was able to spend time with myself and decide how I was going to get through this illness. I learned to set boundaries on my time and myself. I learned about the transformative power of love and forgiveness. I found a deeper understanding of the importance of family. But most of all, I learned how important the journey of healing is for the human psyche. The journey to healing is really a journey of personal growth and growth is an essential part of living. Growth requires adaptation and flexibility and in the shifting tides of life, if we aren't flexible and don't learn to adapt, we become rigid and immovable and eventually we will break.

The healing journey that leads to physical, emotional, mental or spiritual wholeness is unique to each person but along the way, we all go through similar emotions. We all feel afraid and discouraged at times but we also have moments of hope and love. I learned that ultimately, there is more hope than hopelessness and that there is enough love in the world to overcome the fear.

Melissa's

I have always believed in "DIVINE ORDER"—of being at THE place at THE time. You know the "natural" unfolding of events in our lives. In my young adult years I was oblivious to the pain and suffering of others until the pain and suffering I had always seen from "afar" became my own. In the midst of my 18-year active drug addiction, I became estranged from my children, parents, and my younger sister Jennifer. Homelessness became a way of life for me. As I wandered the streets at night, my heart was always heavy with the longing for home and the love of my family. I longed to be the mother, daughter, and "big sister" I should be. Active addiction has a way of changing even the best-laid plans.

However, on October 6, 1993, I got "clean" through a 12-step program known as Narcotics Anonymous. It saved my life and introduced me to me again. I found, through an assignment given to me by my loving "sponsor," what I wanted to be when I grew up! At about nine months clean I began the journey of completing my college education and developing my vision of how I wanted to "go through the world." While in Occupational Therapy school at the Medical College of Georgia, I saw an article entitled, "Center to Help Women with Addiction" and I knew at that moment that I would eventually have a place that would provide a stable living environment for women who are starting their lives "over" as a result of the devastation caused by addiction. Recovery has given me the precious "GIFT" of living two lives in one lifetime. I wanted to share that "GIFT" with other women. Hope is perhaps the greatest miracle that has occurred in my life. With hope, I was able to remain steadfast on my personal healing journey as well as share the gift of hope with others. It is through this "sharing" of love I have been able to pursue my personal dreams and goals.

Upon completion of Occupational Therapy school, I worked in various settings, but in my heart held fast to my dream of opening this place for women. As I would meet people I began to notice how they could possibly fit into my long-term dream. It was as if all the pieces, places, and people were coming together- again in that "DIVINE ORDER" kind of way! My mother, sister, and friends began calling me the "networking queen!" It's true, I was not afraid to ask questions and/or ask others how they saw themselves fitting into my plan. I was surprised how many people stated their interest in working with or for me! Many people I met shared information with me that they normally receive fees for-I attribute their kindness as part of the "DIVINE ORDER" as well. There have been many *Angels* along the way. I moved to Chicago in June of 2000 and everything really began to fall into place. My sister and I had began to have somewhat of a relationship, but not as I had hoped for, but my sponsor continued to encourage me to "keep my side of the street clean!" Today, Jennifer and I have a wonderful relationship, much more beautiful than I could have ever imagined. Her "gifts" are many and complementary to mine. It was inevitable we would make great business partners as well as great friends. Her friendship and growing respect has been the greatest "gift" to come out of our business ventures. This book is the result of the healing which has occurred in my life as well as the relationship with my sister, Jennifer.

My individual healing process has been and is an amazing journey! In early recovery I had my own "personal" test for the 12-step program I am a member of---if I could experience "relief" from one particular hurt in my life-recovery worked! Needless to say, with the application of the Spiritual principles in my life-recovery works!! I have developed a courage which I know must be God-given, as I have faced situations in my life which have left me spiritually, emotionally, physically, and financially bankrupt. My sense of self-worth was destroyed. I felt alone, alienated, and unique. I felt no one could understand my pain. As my drug use changed from social to anti-social, I found I did not even know the person I had become. Gone was the bright-eyed little girl who wanted to be a doctor when she grew up. Gone was the young woman who wanted to be a responsible daughter, mother, sister, and wife. My internal pain was such that I would opt for what I KNEW was only temporary relief just to have ANY relief from my self-made prison. Somehow I could not make the transition from my head to my heart about the need for me to accept personal responsibility for my life and hence my "healing work." It was much easier to blame others and the state of the world for the mess I had made of my life.

> Every day to me was supposed to be special. I demanded and got all the attention that I needed and wanted. My concept of myself at this time was that I was to be cared for the rest of my life, and all I had to do was to be

pretty and smile and the rest would be a piece of cake. I put the responsibility of my existence on everyone but me and if I wasn't happy, they weren't doing their job. Of course when things went my way, I took all the credit. To me, no one knew how to make me happy. I was constantly filled with frustration and anxiety because nothing I did seemed to get me to that place called Happiness.[11]

[11] "A Little Girl Grows Up"- Narcotics Anonymous® Basic Text, page 169

PART II.
THE PRINCIPLES

Chapter 3

Love

"Love makes your soul crawl out from its hiding place."
Their Eyes Were Watching God
Zora Neale Hurston

Love is a healing balm. Used liberally it can cure any ill. But how many of us have the courage to use love in the way that it is meant to be used? How many of us have the courage to use love to heal others and ourselves? More importantly, how do we utilize love to help us heal our physical, emotional, mental and spiritual wounds?

What does it mean to love? What does it *look* like to love oneself? What does it *look* like to love someone else? These are not such difficult questions, yet often we find ourselves acting from a place that is less than loving, especially when it comes to loving ourselves. In order for healing to occur, love must be present. Yet since most people embark on the healing journey from a place of "wounded ness," it is often difficult to see the path to love. When we are in pain, it is hard to feel anything else yet we must move beyond this pain in order to truly be whole again. After all, most people's pain—

emotional, spiritual and even physical revolves around some issue of love: the absence of love; never having been loved; never loving anyone including ourselves; never seeing anyone loved; getting the wrong kind of love; not getting enough love. Until we come to terms with our personal experiences with love, we cannot totally begin to heal. To do this requires that we be honest about our past and current experiences with love and that we be willing to learn to approach and experience love in a different way. But learning to love in a new way requires patience and practice. If we have spent many years being unloved or if we have been unloving to ourselves, coming from a place of love in all of our interactions in the world can seem truly foreign. If we have never experienced love, it may be difficult for us to even recognize love much less put it into practice. So what does "real" love look like?

Love is a word that we throw around in our culture so recklessly that the essence of its meaning gets lost. According to Webster's, love means many things. It is "a strong affection for or attachment or devotion to a person or persons; God's benevolent concern for mankind; and sexual passion or gratification."[12] Yet these are only surface meanings. To understand the true nature of love, one must experience it. Unconditional love for the self or someone else is an intense experience that comprises compassion, openness, honesty and care giving.

To love ourselves unconditionally means that we are gentle with ourselves, allowing ourselves to feel whatever we feel without censure or judgment. This is compassion. Yet we must be honest with ourselves about our behaviors and actions and be open to changing those behaviors that are damaging to others or ourselves. To love others and ourselves we must give care. On a personal level, this means that we respect and take care of our physical, mental and spiritual selves. This means that we eat healthy food, get adequate rest and exercise. It means that we eliminate as much stress in our lives as we can and learn to cope with the stress of which we cannot rid ourselves. To take care of our spiritual self means paying attention to our "inner voice" and

[12] Webster's New Twentieth Century Unabridged Dictionary, 2nd Edition, Prentice Hall, New York, NY

learning to trust the guidance it sends our way. But loving ourselves also means that we seek help when we need it in dealing with issues in each of those arenas of our lives.

To love another person is, in theory, the same as loving one's self. In practice, it can be more difficult because though we can love another person, we cannot control or change who that person is, even though this is what many of us want to do. Accepting another person for who they are is the first, most important and probably the most difficult key to truly loving that person. Instead, we sometimes get caught up in our expectations of what love should be. We expect our beloved to treat us a certain way (even if we've never told them how we want to be treated); we expect our beloved to do certain things in order to "prove their love"; we expect all loves to last forever, so we hold onto relationships well after they have become unhealthy for either of the people involved.

How do we get to this realm of love? Where do we start? If we have had little or no experience with love; have had abusive or tainted love; or have been disappointed by love, it can be difficult to get back on the proverbial horse. But ride again we must, if we want to heal. In order to do this, we must begin in small ways. We can begin to change our ideas about love *simply by wanting to change.* The desire to change our behaviors sparks a flame that, though perhaps tiny at first, can blaze into a roaring fire large enough to burn through even the most difficult times.

Jennifer

There was never an absence of love in my life. I was, from the beginning, a child that had all the accessories of love: a two parent home, a small town upbringing replete with extended family and teachers and schoolmates that remained the same for most of my school career. But somewhere along the way, my notions about what it meant to love *myself* became altered. As many people did, I grew up under what I perceived as unspoken expectations for my behavior, attitude and persona. For many years, I conformed unquestioningly to those expectations. However, as a teenager, I began to question who I really was and as I graduated from high school and went to college, the questions continued and intensified. A man with whom I had a long-term relationship with during this time placed additional expectations on my behavior and it was then that I really had to determine whom I was and what it was that I loved about myself, if anything. For a long time, I couldn't really see anything too much that was lovable. I had "good traits," I suppose: I was intelligent, relatively attractive, and funny—all of the necessities that society said one needed to be loved. But I chose to buy into other people's notions (real or imagined) about who I should be and to me; it appeared as though I wasn't measuring up to those expectations. I began disliking myself for this and this became a pattern. The more I didn't live up to some outside expectation the less love I could show to myself. This meant that I began to really not care about what happened in my life—I was living by default. Moreover, the less love I could show to myself, the less love I could show to others.

After many years of living this way, I began to grow tired. I wanted to feel differently. I wasn't sure what that meant or how I would get there, I just wanted to stop feeling *bad*. I began to re-visit my earliest experiences of love. I tried to remember the things that I had loved about myself when I was a child—before the years of the jaded adolescent. It was a struggle and I had to comb the recesses of my memory to find those things about myself that others and I had found lovable. Once I managed to find one thing that was lovable about me, and they were tiny things at first, such as "Okay, I have nice eyelashes—I can love my eyelashes"—I had a foundation upon which to build. But loving one self on a daily basis is not as easy as it seems. I found myself, especially in the beginning, slipping back into unloving behavior. For a while, this oscillating continued—I went back and forth between loving and hating myself. When I developed cancer some years later, I was still caught up in this "back and forth" self-love. But by then, I was ready to try and fully love myself "24/7/365" and even if I wasn't wholly ready, my illness demanded that I take some control over my life and make some changes or I wouldn't make it. I chose to start loving myself. For me, that means that I say "no" to things that don't feel right to me rather than agreeing to do things out of a sense of obligation or guilt. It means that I care enough about myself to take care of myself physically and most importantly; it means that I give myself "a break." I no longer attempt to adhere to someone else's notions of who I should be. I have come to terms with all of the nuances of my personality and I now truly love them all. Though it is still sometimes a challenge to remain in that "place of love" when dealing with ourselves or other people. We become frustrated about something in our daily routine or we forget to set boundaries and become over-committed and irritable. But even those states of mind can be transformed by love. If we can view our most challenging moments as opportunities to learn something about ourselves then we are acting from a place of love. Rather than "beating ourselves up" we are able to find the positive and embrace it. When we embrace the positive rather than the negative, whether we know it or not, we do already exist in a state of love.

Melissa

When I describe my childhood to people, I tell them that I now know I had a wonderful childhood. Both of my parents were present. My father and I would go fishing or to various sports events. We spent time visiting the elders of the community and our family, and let's not forget the "pool checkers" games I observed on many occasions! My mother and I would go see performances of the Alvin Ailey American Dance Company and Earth, Wind, and Fire in Atlanta. My televised birthday parties on the "Mr. Pix Show" broadcast out of Atlanta were "the bomb" as well! How many children have the experience of celebrating their birthdays on television? I was enrolled in ballet, tap, and drama classes. The list could go on and on. We rented a beach house every summer on Jekyll Island or Cape Cod-life was great! Everything around me was sending the message I was loved. Why was it then that I had this perceived hole as I got older which translated into I was not loved? Somewhere along the way, my definition of love changed. It changed as a result of the disappointments in my life. It changed as a result of my lack of emotional maturity. It changed as a result of "material things" becoming synonymous with love in "my world." It changed because I lost my sense of self and allowed others to define me and my concept of love. It changed when my definition of love was narrowed down to romantic love only, which meant I was "cut-off" from the world as a whole because all I needed was the "right" man and the world could "go to…" When my definition of love no longer included the sometimes-elusive "self-love," I was in a downward spiral going nowhere fast. In *The Alchemy of the Heart* by Reshad Feild writes:

> It is our responsibility to learn how to love. By learning what love is, and its purpose, we will break through the world of illusions into the real world and we will come upon the great secret. [13]

The "great secret" for me was the realization of the connection between my inability to love others and my self-hatred. It was no longer a mystery to me as to why I felt no one loved me. I felt unloved because I was unable to identify love anymore! Love's face had changed so much over the years that it had become unrecognizable. As I traveled the road to self-love I reestablished a relationship with a loving power greater than myself and was spiritually renewed. My journey "back to

---

[13] Field, Reshad *The Alchemy of the Heart,* Elements Books Limited Press: UK

love" began with my recovery work. As I began the journey of self-discovery, I became increasingly capable of expressing a healthier sense of love. It manifested as unconditional. It manifested as service-oriented. It manifested as sacrificial. It manifested as compassionate honesty. It manifested as responsibility for my actions as I "go through the world." I can speak love, but can I "live" love? Staying committed to the healing work over the years has facilitated my ability to "live love."

I thank God for my wonderful loving "sponsors" I have had over the years. It was only in 1993 that I surrendered to the principles of my 12-step program. I had a sponsor briefly early on in my recovery, but our paths diverged. As she left the 12-step program, I connected with a woman who would prove to be an Angel like no other! She taught me things about love, which always began with doing my work in order to be of service to others. One of my first "assignments" was to put a "sticky note" on my bathroom mirror to remind me to tell myself how much I love me! I had about 30 days "clean" and really hated myself at that time. I would fly by the mirror and mumble a quick "I love you Melissa" and keep going! I did not know how profoundly my life would be changed by that simple yet necessary act. I eventually grew to be able to pause and look myself in the eye and smile at me when I spoke those words of self-love aloud! I continue that exercise to this day-11 years later-and the effects are always affirming and sometimes hilarious as I ad-lib and have fun with me! What does this have to do with love? The answer to that is that "if you want to know how I will treat you, watch how I treat me!" Until I developed a love for myself, I was unable to express love for others in a healthy manner. My intolerance and self-loathing would manifest itself in my interactions with others around me. I was miserable and would lash out at the people closest to me. I had to realign myself with others who had a healthy sense of love, ask for help and guidance, make peace with myself, make peace with others, redefine my relationship with God, and go out into the world to be a conduit of love.

In *The Invitation,* Oriah Mountain Dreamer writes that, "It doesn't interest me how old you are. I want to know if you will risk looking like a fool for love, for your dream, for the adventure of being alive."[14]

I have learned that love is about courage. I can remember a time in my life when I would enter into relationships looking for a type of "guarantee" that the outcome will be "happily ever after!" "There is nothing which stings as much as the sting of romantic love's bite! I read somewhere that "as deeply as you love-as deeply you will hurt." That had proven to be my experience. What has changed over recent years is that I am no longer held hostage by the hurts of my past to the extent that will not allow me to risk loving again. When I began my recovery journey love was sex, and sex was "safe" because I could share my love physically without sharing my heart—what an illusion! Time after time I would find myself wondering, "How did I get here" when I was hurting from an unhealthy attachment which I labeled love. However, as my recovery progressed, I finally experienced what it was like to love in a way that meant to accept another person as they are without the "need" to change them-to be

---

[14] Mountain Dreamer, Oriah, *The Invitation*. Harper Collins Publishing: New York, 1999

willing to compromise and not have all the answers. To trust even in the face of my insecure moments and become vulnerable enough to share what I am really feeling without the fear of you leaving me. The boundaries I have learned to set sustain my self-esteem and self-worth. The line has blurred at times, but the truth remains the same. I am still a "work in progress." I strive to honor MY truth about how love is expressed in my life.

The courage I possess has developed primarily from the "evidence" which has accumulated in my life over the years. Beginning the journey of completing college, establishing myself in my career, and becoming a business owner has proven to be a challenge. However, through each experience I learned what works, what does not work, and that there is always room for improvement! I asked a lot of questions, attended a large number of trainings and seminars, and prayed all the time! Some of my most humorous memories are of me in my car alone-talking to my Higher Power aloud about how I feel she is "tripping" regarding my present circumstances! There were many times I was in so much emotional pain that my only consolation was that I knew my Higher Power must really think a lot of me to place the situations before me. I always have what I need to grow through the learning experiences in my life! Everything is always in "Divine Order!" The peace I have in my life helped keep me centered on days when my pain was unspeakable. On the day my sister called me to tell me of her diagnosis in September of 2003, I cried all day. I would call people on the phone to talk about my pain, but nothing would come out except cries of pain. Thank God for my friends because they knew I just needed someone to listen. That same week I had put my youngest son out of the house secondary to his behavior and I was grieving that loss. A romantic relationship was being grieved as well because the commitment to monogamy was broken. Yet, from these experiences I found a deeper relationship with myself through the love of God in my life. There were moments that nothing any human being could say would comfort me. My comfort came from the talks with my Higher Power and the feeling of peace that is within me even in the midst of all that is happening around me.

It is also courage and self-forgiveness that has brought me to a place of peace regarding my role as a mother. Initially, my relationships with my sons, Jeremy and Curt, were formed out of my guilt and shame. I knew I had missed a lot of important moments and years in their life, but I knew I was not living like that any longer. I could now be available and make the most of the moments I had before me. I learned to say "no" and risk their anger and sometimes-harsh words to remind me of what I had done or not done during my active addiction and recovery! Recovery is not an "overnight sensation!" The work in ongoing and I do the best I can as a mother and as a result my relationship with my sons has improved greatly. I love them and I am very proud of the young men they are. My prayer is for them to find their way through life with joy and a great sense of who they are as men.

Patches of Love

- Unconditional love transforms
- Love is honest
- Love is forgiving
- Love is compassionate
- We can begin changing our ideas about love by *desiring the change.*

Chapter 4

Forgiveness

"Forgiveness means letting go of all hope of a better past."

Annie Lamott

In theory, forgiveness is a simple concept but in practice, it can be a bit more challenging. Imagine: there are two little words that can begin the process of forgiveness. But "I apologize," for many people, is one of the most difficult phrases to say. Admitting that we are wrong is hard for most people because it makes us vulnerable. Forgiveness also requires letting go of things that happened in the past. We cannot change the things that happened in the past, we can only come to terms with them and this is the essence of forgiveness.

Here are some important things to remember about forgiveness, though. Grudges can be heavy things to carry around with us. Consider the energy required to keep anger alive. We have to continue to re-visit the incident or issue that sparked the animosity and we have to try to maintain the same levels of animosity for the duration of time in which we are unforgiving. And what if the person that we are not forgiving has moved on with their life and is not even *engaged* any longer in the issue at hand? What if we are still unforgiving to someone who is no longer even living? What are the consequences of this kind of resistance to forgiving?

In her groundbreaking and bestselling work, *Why People Don't Heal and How they Can,* Carolyn Myss writes about the connection between our unwillingness to forgive and our ability to heal:

> The only way to release the pattern into which we have locked ourselves is to release the weight of the past—to get out the energy debt we can no longer afford to carry. Forgiveness is one sure way out of debt. Forgiving does not mean saying that what happened to you doesn't matter, or that it is all right for someone to have violated you. It simply means releasing the negative feelings you have about that event and the person or persons involved.[15]

When viewed in this light, forgiveness is perhaps a little easier to grasp and perhaps a little easier to put into practice.

---

[15] Myss, Carolyn, *Why People Don't Heal and How They Can* Three Rivers Press: New York, 1997.

Jennifer

Forgiveness was a hard thing for me to grasp. Like many people, I really did not like change. I am a creature of comfort and though I like innovative ideas and conversation, I have always secretly enjoyed the order of my routines. We all have our comfort zones.

Over the past ten years, though, I had come to many of the conclusions that Myss makes in terms of the energy that we waste by not forgiving others. But when I encountered the quotation that is at the beginning of this chapter, it changed my whole notion of forgiveness. The quote is so powerful for me: "Forgiveness means letting go of all hope of a better past." For me, this quote puts resentment in its proper perspective. In fact, when I first read this quote, I immediately felt silly for any resentment that I was holding onto. The profundity of the quote is wrapped in its simplicity. It forces us to remember that whatever it is that we are not forgiving is over–it is in the past. Since the past cannot be changed then, we must ask ourselves how much time are we willing to waste on something that is in the unalterable past. For me, I determined that the amount was zero.

Melissa

A powerful quotation from Eastern spiritual traditions is “Hate is a cancer upon the soul.”[16] I remember the time in my life when “hate” was very much a part of my vocabulary and my life. I cannot remember who asked me to remove hate from my vocabulary-I think it was my mother. I used the word to describe my dislike of foods, clothing, people, and many things about myself. I do however, remember how my Spirit began to change when I began to be conscious of how often I used “hate” and found other words to describe my dislikes. I was very unhappy with myself and that unhappiness leaked out onto you if you were around me. I blamed others for the state of my life-which was really just me having to live in

---

[16]Gold, Taro, *Open Your Mind, Open Your Life-A Book of Eastern Wisdom,* Andrews McMeel Publishing: Kansas City

the consequences of MY choices, actions, and decisions! I could not forgive myself or others-I was stuck in anger, resentment, and vengefulness. I plotted in my mind how to make people "pay" for the harm they had caused me-some real, some imagined or blown out of proportion. The price they would have to pay would be emotional, financial, or physical-I became proficient at throwing things!

I was so self-centered that I would be appalled at the notion someone had done or said something to harm me. "Don't they know who I am?" It was a great freedom to move from "Why me?" to "Why not me?" Once again, the credit for moving from a place of hate and unforgiving goes to the recovery "work" which has been done. I found that it was easier to not forgive you so I would not have to do the "work" to forgive me! If I could keep harboring the resentments and hatred, then I could continue to justify-in my mind-the need to escape from the hurt I was carrying.

The shift in my thinking and in my heart came when I realized in my own humanness that others are human as well. Who am I that I cannot forgive? Being human-I too will be seeking forgiveness. The ongoing process of forgiving-myself and others has eased the burden I carried for so many years.

Patches of Forgiveness

- We cannot change the things that happened in the past; we can only come to terms with them.

- When we don't forgive, we use valuable energy holding on to old resentments that we need to instead be using to live fully in the present.

Chapter 5

Hope

"Dream deep for every dream precedes the goal"

Pamela Vaull Starr

Hope is an integral part of the healing journey. Whether we are working on emotional, mental, physical or spiritual healing, we must believe that things can get better. In the absence of hope, we have no motivation to try to improve those things that we can "control" by ourselves nor do we have any faith in our higher power's ability to provide guidance in improving those things that are beyond our control. Whether we fully understand it or not, the universe offers to us a state of grace and this state is where hope lives. Grace is what protects us in a car wreck in which we "should" have been killed. It is our "spiritual safety net" so to speak, and it assures us that we are safe in the infiniteness that is our higher power. If we can remember to connect to that state of saving grace then we can maintain a sense of hope.

Hope also allows us to tap into the possibilities of the future. It is the fuel of our dreams. It allows us to see the positive potential in any situation. It gives us permission to do or be something that we have not done or been in the past. Hope is akin to imagination because if we can imagine a thing, then that means that we are able to visualize the scenario in which our imaginings occur. Once we are able to visualize our dreams, then we are able to take steps toward achieving those dreams. When we begin down the path towards whatever we have imagined hope is the thing that keeps us focused on our goal. In *Love, Medicine and Miracles*, Bernie Siegel talks about the power of hope to bring change to our lives. He writes:

> ... Meditation and visualization are powerful tools to help you be aware of your true needs and then make them happen. Seeing what you want in your mind's eye helps convince your unconscious that it's possible, and that helps create an atmosphere of hope.[17]

Still hope can be an elusive concept. We may be able to place a dictionary definition on the word but putting hope into action is something else altogether.

---

[17]Siegel, Bernie S., *Love, Medicine and Miracles* Harper Perennial: New York, 1990

When we think of a hopeful person, we think of someone who is the cheerful optimist. This is the "glass-is-half-full" person that can seemingly find something good in every situation. But how do these people come to this place in their lives? How are they able to see only positives in a world that is so full of negativity? The answer lies in our ability to choose.

The difference between hope and despair is centered on our chosen perspective. Perspective is simply the willingness to see a situation from a different angle. When we are trying to heal some part of ourselves it can often be difficult to find even a small spark of hope. In these moments we can be reminded that not only do we exist in a forgiving and loving universe we also exist in a community of human beings, many of whom have undertaken similar healing journeys. We can be inspired by these experiences. Sometimes it can be difficult to discover within ourselves, the hope necessary to pull us from the brink of despair. But we must be patient with ourselves and we must persevere in our quest for hope. Because in the absence of hope there is only despair and despair keeps us imprisoned in the patterns and beliefs of the past but hope frees us to the potentiality of tomorrow.

Jennifer

Hope was a particularly difficult thing for me to grasp. Since I suffered from depression for many years, hopelessness was a way of life for me and this didn't really change until I developed cancer. In *Love, Medicine and Miracles*, Siegel talks about the connection between depression and hopelessness and the development of cancer.

> Feeling that present conditions and future possibilities are intolerable, the depressed person "goes on strike" from life, doing less and less, and losing interest in people, work, hobbies and so on. Such depression is strongly linked with cancer... Many people, however, continue on with their routines and an outward show of happiness, when on the inside their lives have come to lack all meaning. These persons are seldom diagnosed as clinically depressed, because they manage to keep functioning. Their state is the "quiet desperation" of James Thurber's Walter Mitty meek and obliging on the outside,

> but filled with unacknowledged rage and frustration.[18]

This resonated so strongly with me. It described how I had been feeling for so long and to think that this state of mind could have in any way contributed to the illness that I was now experiencing was mind blowing. It made me completely shift the way I thought about life. Now I don't wish to imply that I went from being a depressed person to being a cheerful, optimistic person overnight. I had forgotten what it meant to be hopeful and really didn't know where to start. Where was I going to get hope? What I did know was that I wasn't going to succumb to this illness. I was going to get through it and learn from it but I wasn't going to succumb. If this meant being hopeful, I was willing to give it a try. At first, my attempts felt phony—they *were* phony. Doubt and fear and frustration would creep in on my fragile hope and I would have to battle to remain hopeful. I discovered that it was easier and less stressful to live hopefully than hopelessly. I came to understand that

[18] Siegel, Bernie S. *Love, Medicine and Miracles*, Harper Perennial: New York, 1990.

I had reason to be hopeful because our higher power offers us grace. When I began to understand this I started to cultivate grace. In moments when I felt particularly low during my physical healing, I would ask for more strength to handle all of the emotions or pain that I was going through and from some place inside of me, I would find the endurance to go on. I came to understand this as the state of grace and I learned to appreciate grace because it surely sustained me when I was in the bowels of despair.

Melissa

"Never, never, never give up"
Winston Churchill

Hope changed my life. As a matter of fact, hope saved my life. I had reached a point in my life where I felt hopeless. I was homeless for about five years. My relationship with my children, parents, sister, and other friends and loved ones was non-existent. I weighed 89 pounds and was eating food off the ground that someone had dropped. I was sleeping in abandoned buildings during the winter and summer. But I feared other people coming into those buildings to rob or...more than I feared the elements. I felt God was punishing me so I had no hope left that I could reclaim my life. The introduction of a 12-step program into my life in 1984 changed my life. I could no longer use drugs without the knowledge in the back of my mind that I did not have to live the way I was living. I had heard the stories of how others had changed their lives through recovery. I saw how my own life changed when I applied the principles in my own life. But I was not ready to fully commit to the "work" that had to be done to stay in the recovery process. Hence, my struggle continued because I continued to struggle instead of "letting go" and following suggestions.

I met a woman in 1992-her name was Hope! She became my Spiritual guide through the 12-steps after I returned to recovery in 1993. For over ten years she continued to encourage, support, confront, and love me. It was my first experience with unconditional love that I was in a state where I could receive it with open-mindedness. She was named Hope and she gave me hope. I am eternally grateful to her. As I began to get a glimpse of hope it grew like wildfire and I have never lost hope since that time in my life. If I had not one dime in my pocket today-I still have hope. Hope has given me the courage to attempt to "live the life I have imagined!"

Patches of Hope

- Hope comes when we understand that we exist in a state of saving grace.

- Grace is the unconditional acceptance that our higher power offers to us.

- Hope allows us to tap into the possibilities of the future.

Chapter 6

Trust

"You must do the thing you think you cannot do."

Eleanor Roosevelt

Trust comes when we are able to recognize and respect the synchronicity of life. We have all had the experience of being in just the right place at just the right moment to seize and opportunity or meet the right person. Or perhaps you awaken one morning and have a question or issue about which you need or want more information and then later that day as you happen to be watching TV, they feature a report on the issue or you have a conversation with a friend where your question is answered without you having even asked it—your friend just says the information you need seemingly "out of the blue." If we pay attention to these kinds of moments, we will notice a pattern. Learning to flow with these "coincidences" often leads us to wonderful opportunities, people and experiences. This is trust.

Trust requires that we give up the need for specific outcomes in a situation. Trust requires that we learn to be still and listen to that voice inside of us and to pay attention to what that voice is saying. In time, as we learn to focus more on that inner guidance, the guidance becomes clearer and we are able to see that all along, "something" has been guiding our steps. Whether you call this something "God," "a higher power," "the Divine," or "the universe" is inconsequential. What is important to remember is that it is the immense, underlying force that connects us all does have order and plans "and whether or not it is clear to you, no doubt the universe is unfolding as it should."[19] In other words, we must come to understand that all of the coincidences in our lives have something to teach us about ourselves and use those moments to try and discover what those lessons are.

How does it feel when we trust the flow of life? If you trust the flow of life you feel calm, "centered," and relaxed. If you feel uptight or tense, you are worried. Do not mistake concern for worry. Worry is the opposite of trust. It depletes the mental, emotional and spiritual resources that we need to be focusing, instead, on our healing. But to

---

[19]Ehrmann, Max, *Desiderata*, 1952

trust does not mean that we are no longer concerned about the things that happen in our lives. When we are able to trust life, we may become concerned about events in our lives or people's behavior but we don't allow that concern to take over our lives. We are able to place events in a larger context and move forward.

There are other elements of trust. It is the foundation for our personal relationships. We have degrees of trust for people based on what role they occupy in our lives. We trust our colleagues to carry out their job responsibilities. We trust our family and friends to be honest with us and to offer us support when needed and we trust other people at different junctures in our lives with our personal, mental and emotional well-being. Yet how do we develop these levels of personal trust? More importantly, what do we do when this kind of trust is violated?

Some types of trust are granted just by nature of the relationship. Familial bonds essentially have "built-in trust." Children instinctively trust their parents and siblings and other close family relations generally trust each other. Figures of authority also garner a certain amount of general trust. In recent years, scandals concerning corrupt government leaders, police officers and clergy have made us cautious about extending this kind of blanket trust to people in authority but nevertheless, we all still tend to believe that most people in authority can be trusted.

Other levels of personal trust are developed over time. People with whom we have regular interactions demonstrate their trustworthiness to us by their behavior and we do likewise. Eventually, after enough demonstrated trustworthy behavior (the specific amount varies for each of us) we reach a level of comfort with that person that allows us to extend our trust to them.

Occasionally, we trust people "on the spot." We get a "good feeling" about a person or think that they have a "trustworthy face" or "honest eyes." Whether or not these impressions turn out to be accurate or not depend in large part on how in tune one is with one's inner guidance. However, it is important to remember that genuine trust is developed because of we become comfortable with a person's pattern of behavior.

When trust is abused, it is often difficult to extend ourselves in that way again. But in order to be a healthy human being we must interact with other human beings and this requires a degree of trust. Therefore, we must not allow ourselves to become jaded because we may have lost our sense of trust. Instead, we should try to learn from our experience—why and how was my trust violated? What part did I play in this experience and what can I do to prevent similar occurrences in the future? When we have taken this kind of inventory, we will be more aware of those behaviors that make people untrustworthy and so hopefully be able to avoid those kinds of people and interaction. Moreover, we will be more keenly aware of the flow of life and learn to trust that the currents of life are always carrying us in the right direction.

Jennifer

I have always been a person who valued the mind and all that it could tell us. The tangibility of the "knowledge" that our intellect could help us to discover was comforting to me. So learning to trust an intangible something "higher than or larger than" me seemed, at times, far-fetched. It wasn't that I couldn't see a certain order to the universe. I could even conceive that there might be a plan to the whole thing. But to just "have faith" in this something, to believe that I could or should just turn over every facet of my life to this unknowable just didn't make much sense. I wanted more "proof." So I spent my college years looking for some viable evidence of this higher power in which I was supposed to feel confident in placing my trust. I discovered many different theories on the existence of a higher power but it wasn't until I began to see glimpses of this "power" working in my life that I began to release the need for tangible proof. There were only small coincidences at first and then more extended moments of synchronicity. Eventually, I gave up the need to "have proof" of the divine. Ironically, when I did this, I recognized its presence in my life even more.

At the same time, I worked on issues of personal trust in my life. I am the kind of person who tends to trust a person until they give me reason not to. However, as I maneuvered through the world, I encountered some untrustworthy people and I had to learn to interact with these people while not allowing their behavior to affect me. Additionally, people who were close to me—intimate family and friends sometimes violated the trust that I had in them or displayed untrustworthy behavior and I had to learn how to cope with those relationships and work through the resentment and anger that often springs up where there is a lack of trust. This was no easy task. When your trust in someone has been compromised, it feels like a supreme violation because to trust someone means that you place your confidence in that person's ability to act with integrity and do the things to which they commit.

For a long time, for me, if I lost trust in someone, it was all over. They could never regain that confidence. However as I went through different phases of personal growth, I began to examine my own behavior and saw many instances where I had acted with less integrity than I would have liked. Once I was able to admit this about myself, I was able to develop more compassion for other people and in this way I could begin to understand why they exhibited some of those untrustworthy behaviors.

Admittedly, I still encounter untrustworthy people but now I pay attention to my inner guidance. When a "red flag" goes up about a person's integrity or motives, I heed the message and protect myself in whatever ways are necessary. In listening to this guidance, I am practicing the act of trusting life in general and I have discovered that when you begin to trust life you release expectations and surrender the need to control outcomes. You accept that life has a plan and that there is a lesson to be learned in every encounter.

Melissa

> "One may defeat a thousand obstacles and adversaries, yet he who defeats the enemies within is the noblest victor."
>
> Shakyamuni

Many of the trust "issues" I thought I had were born out of my own lack of trustworthiness. I lived in fear of someone doing to me what I had done to them. I believed in "you reap what you sow," therefore I entered into all relationships "waiting for the ball to drop." I felt no one was to be trusted. I hid out behind "I can't trust people anymore." That rationalization allowed me to "play it safe" and I did so by not engaging in healthy relationships because of my fears of being hurt or becoming vulnerable. My motto became, "I will get them before they get/reject me!" My relationships, (platonic or romantic), were sabotaged from the very beginning.

The shift came when I became aware of the depth of my fears and how I had become a prisoner in my "self-made prison." It was as if I wanted a crystal ball to show me what the future would bring regarding my various relationships. I have a dear friend who has reminded me of my addiction to certainty!

I was faced with continuing to exist without fully experiencing human interactions based on mutual respect and trust or begin to trust and be MY best in the relationship regardless of others' behavior. Once I began to trust, love flowed through my life fully and freely. True victory comes from the defeat of the enemy within.

Patches of Trust

- Trust comes when we are able to recognize and respect the synchronicity or "coincidences" of life.

- Trust requires that we give up the need for specific outcomes in a situation.

Chapter 7

Community

"It's the friends you can call at 4 a.m. that matter."
Marlene Dietrich

Someone said, "No man is an island," even though when we are going through emotional, physical or spiritual healing, we can feel very much like an island: lost in a sea of frustration, uncertainty and confusion. Having a community of family and friends to support us when we need it most is crucial. Since healing is a process that requires many changes in our lives and these changes are often in many different areas of our lives we may develop different emotional and physical needs. Members of our community are often those people that we turn to in order to support these evolving needs.

What does a community look like? It would be easier to describe community in terms of how it feels. Community is anywhere that you feel nurtured and surrounded with love and support. A community may be a group of several people or it may be a close-knit group of 2 or 3 but the commonality is the sustenance that it offers its members.

A community may be found anywhere and most of us are members of multiple communities: families, religious organizations, social groups, and employment settings are all places of community. We belong to some of these groups by circumstance but most communities we join by choice.

Once we are a part of a community we must actively contribute because a community is only as good as its members. We must act individually in ways that will benefit the collective. In Western society, the concept of "community" goes in and out of vogue. Social Darwinism has pervaded our institutions to the extent that many of us are still functioning with the notion of "rugged individualism" as our model for public interaction. But humans are naturally social creatures and so to live as though the individual is all that matters is really counter-intuitive.

Jennifer

I have never really felt as though I belonged to any particular community. Since I grew up in a small town, I was more than familiar with the close-knit sense of community that other people talked about. Growing up, I had observed the behavior of my parents who both grew up in the small town in which we resided. For them, community meant that everyone knew you as well as most people in the two preceding generations of your family. It meant that people came to the need of others and helped each other out in any way that they could. But for my generation, these sensibilities had begun to be somewhat "old-fashioned." Sure, as a part of a small town I was a part of the community and I did benefit from that kind of nurturing environment. For example, I went to school with the exact same group of kids for 12 years. All of our teachers knew our parents on a *very* personal level so there was a sense of having multiple "surrogate" parents. Plus, this left little room for misbehavior. As I grew older, however, I began to view the "nurturing" as "nosiness" and I started to resent the inquisitive nature of neighbors. I began to realize that though I did belong to a community, what I was missing was a sense of "like-mindedness." In the small town where I grew up, I began to feel increasingly out of step.

As I moved out into the world, went to college and started experimenting with the notion of work, I expected to find droves of people who shared my viewpoints and were as smart as I thought myself to be. I believed that once these kindred spirits were discovered that I could simply add water to have an instant community. Mostly, this was true. I experimented with being a part of the university community, found commonalities with people that I worked with and formed transitory communities with the associates that came through my life. But these communities were never full of the sustaining energy present in positive communities.

When I was coping with cancer, I had to reach out to my family and friends. I needed help at times to deal with the physical and mental toll that an extended illness can take. During this time, I came to understand that community is not about the quantity of people involved but rather the quality of their interactions. Communities are started because of the common interests or goals of its members.

But they are sustained by the love and concern that the members show to each other.

My primary community is now comprised of a small group of close friends and family members with whom I share many common interests and concerns. I also belong to other communities that center on other areas of interest to me. I have come to understand that community is a necessary part of being human and I strive to connect with like-minded people whenever possible. But unlike the past, when I would participate in a community just for the sake of doing so, I have learned to be more discriminating. In so doing becoming a part of real communities that help to sustain me when I need it most.

Melissa

> We should think of ourselves in community with everything around us at all times. We should regard people, animals, trees, rivers, even mountains in the same light as ourselves and realize that we all have much in common. Such thoughts cause us to imagine, "If I were in their (or its) place, how would I feel, or what would I do?" Sympathetic

> interaction naturally occurs when we regard other people and things in this way, as part of ourselves, as one of our own kind. When we place ourselves in the position of other people or objects and feel we share their experiences, positive actions arise for all concerned, both for people and their environment.[20]

It's ironic to me that my sense of community began to surface again during my active addiction. I had learned from my parents as I was growing up, in deed and word, the importance of acknowledging the condition of others and doing your part to end the oppression. However, it was a different story when I was the one who could only get clean clothes by going to the clothes bank at the community church. There was a Thanksgiving I spent standing in a line outside of a church in Albany, Georgia to get a holiday dinner. At first, I was so embarrassed. But it was not long before I too knew the meal schedule at the local "soup kitchens." There was a sense of community however, that grew out of our

[20] Gold, Taro, *Open Your Mind, Open Your Life-A Book of Eastern Wisdom,* Andrews McMeel Publishing: Kansas City

hunger and homelessness. People looked out for each other. We would ask around if someone was missing for a day or two. We would share food but not the drugs! I became a part of a community of people who were oppressed by our own hands, but there was additional "extraneous" oppression that came from the mouths of the service providers and "church people" in the form of harsh, stigmatizing, unforgiving words. I felt so detached from the "mainstream." I was no longer connected to my family, nor did I even have a sense of family outside of the people I "used" with. I carried my family in my heart at all times-I was just too ashamed to go home to face my parents and my children.

After I entered into recovery, my sense of community changed. The fellowship helped me to feel "a part of" again in a positive way. I got involved in service work and connected with the feeling of doing for others without expecting anything in return. What a change from the condition of my Spirit when I came into recovery! It was about what YOU could do for ME and that was it! As I began to integrate back into society, my sense of self-worth grew because I learned I was valuable as well as others around me-we all have our "gifts" to contribute.

The next epiphany would occur when I entered the Master of Arts in Community Development program at North Park University in Chicago. Never in my life had I been surrounded by so many "like-minded" people regarding community and how we "go through the world." I knew I had found a safe place because I had been feeling alone in my outrage at the state of the world. I was very vocal about it and my friends were used to my rather militant conversations about what I was doing or would be willing to do. The program at North Park University gave me the added mortar to my foundation. In my first class I met a group of students-Mona, Bridgette, Cheryl, Ron, Mike, Bryan, Diane, Katie, Wiley, and Juliette T. -who would impact me as well. We became a community within our class and travel through life together through our passion to effect change through action and not just words. We are all very different, but very much the same. To my classmates I say, "I love you and thank you for all that you give to me. Thank you for accepting me as I am." To my instructors at

North Park University, thank you for giving me the courage and the knowledge to "go through the world as if it is the way I envision it to be." You have all been a great part of my healing process and expansion of my sense of "community." I now feel "as one" with the world around me.

Patches of Community

- Community is anywhere that you feel nurtured and surrounded with love and support.

- Community is not about the quantity of people involved but rather the quality of their interactions with each other.

Chapter 8

Solitude

"Fond as we are of our loved ones, there comes at times during their absence an explained peace"

Anne Shaw

Being alone is an important part of the healing process. Though we need and appreciate the support of our family and friends, we must have time to ourselves to think, to love ourselves and to integrate all of the experiences that the healing journey brings. Solitude is especially important for women who often have complex emotional and spiritual issues and require time alone to contemplate and silence our minds.

Some may view cultivating solitude as being "selfish." Sometimes, people may take our desire or need to be alone as a personal insult. When we are in the process of healing our family and friends want to support us. But sometimes, other people's ideas of how best to provide emotional or physical support to us are based upon their own ideas about how they would want to be supported in a similar situation. Generally, our family and friends have the best intentions. We simply need to be clear when expressing our need for solitude so that people close to us understand the reasons that we require "alone time." We should explain to our family and friends that our need for solitude is not about "keeping them out" but rather about "letting ourselves in." We can help them to understand that we have to be alone at times in order to make sense of the events in our lives.

Yet solitude is not about the need to "get away from it all." Even though it is about finding a place of retreat, it is not necessarily about a *physical* place. Though many of us do find solace in natural environments and can go to these areas for a planned period of renewal, solitude is a space and place in time in which we can be alone with our thoughts and ourselves. If we are learning to forgive others, and ourselves working through trust issues or just being more self-loving, solitude is the space in which we can feel safe in doing so.

Jennifer

When I was dealing with my illness, I spent a great deal of time alone. Certainly, I spent more time alone than my family and friends were comfortable with. But for me, I needed to have time to try and figure out what lessons this illness had to teach me. It was inevitable that I ask the question "Why me?" but I had to try to figure out an answer that would allow me to move on with my life. It was difficult to do this kind of introspection in the presence of people who, though they loved you and tried to disguise their worry, could suffocate you with their suppressed concern.

I have always liked alone time but for the few year prior to my diagnosis, I had lead an overly committed and stressful lifestyle: I had a teaching job that required a 2 hour round trip daily commute, I was in graduate school and I was teaching a class at a community college. All of these commitments left me little time for myself. I would try to carve out some part of every day as my own though I was often too tired in those precious moments to do anything but rest and though solitude is about resting, it is also about BE-ing. "Quality Solitude" is about having the time and space in which to just live and think and dream and play. I was not enjoying this level of solitude.

Having cancer forced me to realize that I had to take better care of myself. I needed to pay more attention to my emotional and spiritual needs and spending time alone was one of the primary ways that I could begin to give myself this kind of care. I began to cultivate solitude. I started setting aside time to be alone. I would watch mindless TV or read or whatever. Today, solitude is the one thing that I don't neglect ever. I turn off all of the flashing and beeping devices that keep me wired to the outside world and pamper myself at home for an hour or two on a daily basis. I have come to understand that if I don't take that time for myself, I stand the risk of losing that self in all of the routines and absurdities of life.

Melissa

"My wealth is determined by my inner health"

Melissa H.

Being alone was what I disliked most. It was in the quiet moments alone that the "voices" of disgust, self-loathing, and insecurity would become louder. In the "alone time" I would come face to face with the feelings I was trying so hard to anesthetize. As the years went by I found I could feel alone even in a crowd.

There is a difference in the solitude I crave now and the loneliness of years ago. I feared the quiet time-I had to stay busy. I did not want to stop long enough to take notice of the state of my life. I am busy now, but I make the time to meditate, pray, and spend with myself. I am not busy today trying to escape my reality. I am busy today because I am on the cusp of great things and it is requiring a great commitment of time. However, this state is temporary. Projects are being completed, school is almost finished, and the book is about to be hot off the press! Balance is very important to my being. Without solitude being a priority in my life, there would be no balance. I have to spend time with me to keep in touch with me. In the solitude I listen-and my Spirit talks.

My Spirit is richer and more beautiful today as a direct result of the healing work that is ongoing in my life. I continue to love, learn, work, play, and celebrate all aspects of the woman that I am. I love to laugh. Laughter enriches my soul. My Spirit is free to dance and sing. I am present and I know who I am-today. Solitude soothes my soul and enables me to receive all that life may bring to me.

Patches of Solitude

- Solitude is a space and place in time in which we can be alone with our thoughts and ourselves.

- We must practice cultivating solitude in a world often full of noise and distractions.

Chapter 9

Patience

"We could never learn to be brave and patient if there were only joy in the world."

Hellen Keller

Healing is not an event that happens in our lives. It is not a singular moment. It is a process that means that it is ongoing. We must be patient with ourselves and let the healing process happen. Being patient means *allowing.* Allowing means granting enough time and providing adequate space for whatever may occur.

In a world consumed with instant gratification, gathering patience can be a challenge. If we are focused on healing ourselves, we may be consciously aware of our need to be patient but our desire to want to heal is so strong that we forget to allow the process to take place. We are inclined to want everything right now and our desire for the "healing miracle" is no different. We expect people and situations to flow exactly like we want and we get frustrated when this does not occur.

Developing patience for ourselves is even more difficult. Since we are at the center of our healing process, this then is a crucial issue. If we cannot develop and maintain patience with ourselves, our process can become quite involved. But when we are journeying towards wholeness, we must slow down. In fact, often the issues that prompted our healing journey in the first place are usually signposts that give notice to the fact that we are doing too much, moving too fast or we not paying attention to some important element in our lives. If we try to rush through the healing process, we may run the risk of "partial" healing and if our goal is ultimately to be "whole" then we must permit the pieces to all fall into place.

Jennifer

I have never been a particularly patient person. When I graduated from high school, one of my teachers who knew me particularly well reminded me to try to be "more tolerant of people who were not as smart, talented or stylish as me" She said that they "may have something else to offer." It took me many years to truly understand and appreciate the comment. At the time, I thought that she meant was that I was an intolerant, arrogant fool but instead, I came to realize that she was trying to teach me something about how to get along in the world.

Often we are intolerant of things over which we have little or no control: the line at the grocery store or the sloth-like movements of rush hour traffic and being impatient in these instances is an exercise in futility. Yet when we turn our critical eye inward, we can be just as unforgiving and our individual selves are the one thing over which we have certain contr

For me, criticizing myself was almost a full time job. I let outside expectations cloud my vision of whom I could be for a very long time and in light of these expectations I could never feel as though I measured up. When I became ill, all of that changed almost instantly. I no longer had time to be impatient with myself. My body was demanding that I slow down if I was going to overcome this sickness. Additionally, I had to give up my frustration at things that I could not control. I began to learn to control my responses to situations.

I began to practice compassion. These are the essential elements of patience for me.

Certainly, I still lose my patience in traffic or during long, boring meetings but I have learned to put a spin on it. I at the impatience that I am experiencing and try to determine if there's a different response that I could be having or if there is a message in the state of impatience itself. Sometimes our impatience is a clue that we are in a situation that no longer serves us. But I have learned that the key to discovering the potential message in our impatient and intolerant moments is... well, patience. Ahhh, there's the rub.

Melissa

"When the student is ready, the teacher will appear."

Buddhist proverb

Patience is definitely a virtue! I was self-centered, self-seeking, and self-righteous-can go there today if I do not remain vigilant about the condition of my Spirit! I wanted things to go my way and to happen right now! I had no concept of "in God's time." I felt that a Higher Power must be cruel or punishing me if things did not go my way at the time I expected them to happen. Immature does not begin to explain the manner in which I interacted with the world. Most of my disappointment in life was self-inflicted because of the unreasonable expectations I placed on people and situations. I would have everything planned out in my head as to the outcome including when it was supposed to happen.

I developed more patience as I learned to surrender the illusion of control, do the "footwork," and pray for knowledge and acceptance of a "Higher Power's" will in my life. As my trust has grown, I can relax and enjoy the journey more. I am not exerting energy worrying about the future. I can be fully present and accounted for in this moment. As I practice patience in various situations, I find my stress level decreased, people find me pleasant to be around, and I have a more positive outlook on my life.

Patches of Patience

- Healing is a process.
- Processes require time and space in which to occur.
- Patience means giving up our need to control that process.

Chapter 10

Personal Responsibility

"My will shall shape the future. Whether I fail or succeed shall be no man's doing but my own. I am the force; I can clear any obstacle before me or I can be lost in the maze. My choice; my responsibility; win or lose, only I hold the key to my destiny."

Elaine Maxwell

In order to move toward wholeness, we have to learn to move beyond the challenges in our lives. The bad things that we all go through are designed to teach us something about our lives or ourselves. But until we take personal responsibility for the conditions in our lives, we can't move beyond them.

For some the notion of personal responsibility is burdensome. The idea that we are accountable for our actions is off putting to those who would blame someone or something else for all of their problems. If you have spent years relating to the world in this way, assuming personal responsibility can also be frightening. To shift from a place of dependency to independence is a huge transformation but in order to heal, we must enter that particular cocoon.

In reality, personal responsibility is one of the most freeing concepts for one's personal growth. It is true that responsibility does require commitment, honesty and integrity. Yet at the crux of personal responsibility is *choice.* Once we understand the connection between these two, the texture of our lives changes dramatically.

Each moment of our lives is pregnant with potential. We make choices in each moment that bring that potentiality closer to fruition. Our lives are simply a series of these moments and in this way we can see that the choices we make today affect the experiences that we have tomorrow or next month. Surely we can all recall instances when we were able to connect an event—good or bad—to a singular choice from the past. In recognizing those connections we are seeing personal responsibility in action. If we are able to take this one step further and realize that the choice we made in the past could have been different, then we have begun to uncover the freedom inherent in choosing. When we recognize the freedom of choice that we have in each moment, personal responsibility becomes exciting and we begin to understand that we can be the architects of our lives. We *are* the architects of our lives. Whether or not we make our choices consciously, that is fully aware of all of the issues involved, we nevertheless choose. Even making no choice is a choice. It simply means that you are choosing to live a reaction-based life, responding as best you can to whatever life throws your way. But to live and choose with the awareness that your choices affect your future gives us immense power to create the life that we imagine.

Jennifer

Like many people, I spent some time playing "the blame game." All that was going wrong with me was my parent's fault, my man's fault or my somebody-other-than-me's fault.

I began to make the shift from blaming others when I decided that even though other people may have done things to me, I was spending more time blaming them than I was in trying to fix whatever the problem was.

In all of my forays into different systems of personal growth, I began to come across this notion of assuming personal responsibility. It sounded theoretically intriguing but I wasn't sure that any *real* people were out there in the world taking personal responsibility for their actions. I began to toy with the idea of living in this way. As I began to see the connections between my choices and my life, I started to see the power of personal responsibility. Granted, I continued to make choices that were not in my best interest for a while, knowing that these choices would have consequences but I was either willing to deal with them I was unconcerned about the possible ramifications.

The "Big C" changed all that, as I was able to see the direct result of me neglecting my health for so many years. The price that I paid for those choices was a bit high: I underwent surgery and am now unable to have children. But the lessons that I learned were invaluable and have caused a complete shift in my life. Overcoming that particular challenge has made me cognizant of every choice that I make and I now undertake decision making with an eye toward how a particular choice will fit into the life that I want to create for myself.

Melissa

> Everybody can be great, because anybody can serve. You don't have to have a college degree to serve. You don't have to make your subject and your verb agree to serve. You don't have to know about Plato and Aristotle to serve. You don't have to know Einstein's Theory of Relativity to serve. You don't have to know the second theory of thermo-dynamics in physics to serve. You only need a heart full of grace. A soul generated by love.
>
> Reverend Martin Luther King Jr.

One thing is very clear to me now-the majority of my problems were created out of my "inability to accept personal responsibility." It was much easier to blame everyone around me, including the world in general for the state of my life. I was living in a world of "if, but, and should have." When others rejected the idea that they were my problem, I immediately alienated them by further denying any role in my horrid life at that time. I was angry, resentful, irresponsible, and self-centered.

It would take loving parents, a loving sponsor, and loving members of Narcotics Anonymous® to confront my denial and tell me the truth no matter what! Initially I was not open to suggestions about taking responsibility for my life. Yet, as I became more open-minded, I found the responsibility I had avoided would actually increase my sense of independence once I assumed a role in my life. My sense of self-worth grew. I no longer felt as if I had to live my life in the manner I felt you wanted me to because I was being responsible for me, not my parents or some man. It is amazing how people will help you when you are trying to help yourself! It feels great to know my children look at me as trying to be a responsible parent today. My employers can count on me being more responsible today.

As I practice these principles in my life today, I am living a life transformed from degradation to a state of grace and healing. I have received the greatest gift and that is to be able to be of service as I go through my life and understand the personal responsibility that accompanies that gift.

Patches of Personal Responsibility

- Personal responsibility means that we be accountable for our actions

- Assuming personal responsibility gives us the power to create the life that we imagine.

Appendix A

Make your own Miniature Quilt
"Love is On the Horizon"

Figure 1 below is a design that is meant to be made into a quilt square 8.5 inches x 11 inches. The quilt may be made using fabric or paper and basic instructions and patterns follow for making both.

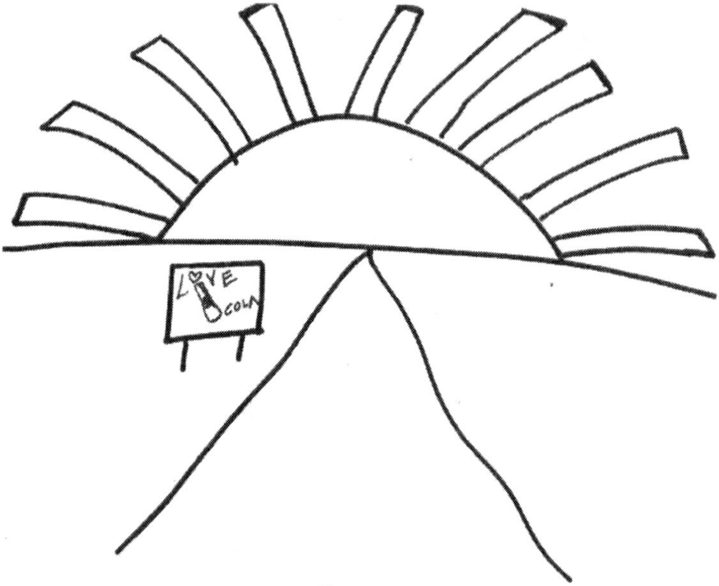

Figure 1

Figure 2 shows the placement for the corresponding pattern pieces.

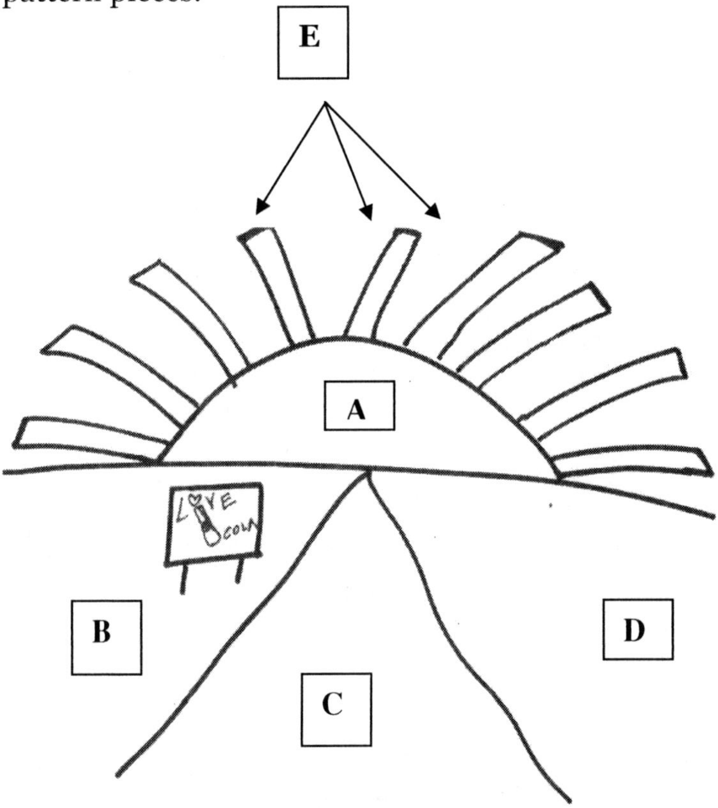

Note: The rays of the sun [E] may be made out of strips of fabric but can just as easily be made from pieces of ribbon or yarn.

Materials and Supplies

For Fabric Quilt

***Note about choosing fabric**: Buy or collect fabric that appeals to you. You'll be looking at your quilt square so make it pleasing to your eyes! Roaming around in your local fabric store will spark ideas. Don't be afraid to choose patterned fabrics as well.*

8.5 x 11 fabric for background

- Look for fabrics that have clouds on them or are a pretty shade of "sky blue"

8x8 inch piece of fabric for the road or path [C]

- We suggest things in the brown or yellow for this

2 6x 6 inch pieces of fabric for the grass/fields on the side of the road [B] and [D]

- Choose fabric that appeals to your ideas about what a field would look like if you were driving into the sunset of this design.

Heat bonded fusable web (your local fabric stores can assist you with this fabulous stuff that will make your life much much easier!)
Sharp Scissors
Iron and Ironing Board (or clean flat surface and thick towel)
Additional items to be used for embellishment:

- Ribbon, yarn or colored string
- Fabric paint
- Interesting or fun buttons and sequins

For Paper Quilt

8.5 x11 sheet of paper for background—the paper may be white or colored depending on your fancy!
Several Sheets of Colored Paper
Markers, Colored Pencils, Paint
Glue
Scissors
Glitter, sequins, buttons and any other fun embellishments

REMEMBER: THIS IS A FUN, CREATIVE PROJECT SO *Have Fun!!!*

Instructions

Whether you choose to do the fabric or the paper version of the quilt square, the instructions are basically the same. The patterns that follow should be copied onto sturdy paper and then cut out.

1. Choose your background fabric or paper
2. Transfer the patterns from this book onto sturdy paper
3. Cut out your patterns
    - If using fabric, iron on the fusable heat bond to fabric following manufacturer's instructions ***PRIOR*** to cutting out patterns on fabric.
4. Cut out patterns from paper or fabric of your choice. Be sure to allow yourself ¼ to ½ inch "trim" around the edges for overlap.
5. Using the lettered diagram, piece the fabric or paper together on the background fabric to make sure of the positioning.
6. Transfer the "pieces" to the background.
    - If using fabric, iron the cut out fabric pieces to the background material.
    - If using paper, glue the pieces onto background paper.
7. Add embellishments to your square:
   Will you make your sun rays out of ribbon or fabric paint?
   Will you use glitter to sparkle up your paper square?
   Will you add "clouds" to your sky by cutting out cloud shapes from white fabric or paper?
   Will you create your own "love billboard" for the side of the road?
8. Finish the edges of the individual pieces.
    - Outline them with ribbon or fabric paint if you're using fabric. If you are ambitious, you can use corresponding colored thread and use simple, closely looped stitches to finish.
    - If using paper, outline the edges in paint, markers or colored pencils.
9. Sign your name on your masterpiece!

Patterns

Copy the patterns onto heavy paper. It will be easier to use the patterns with the fabric.

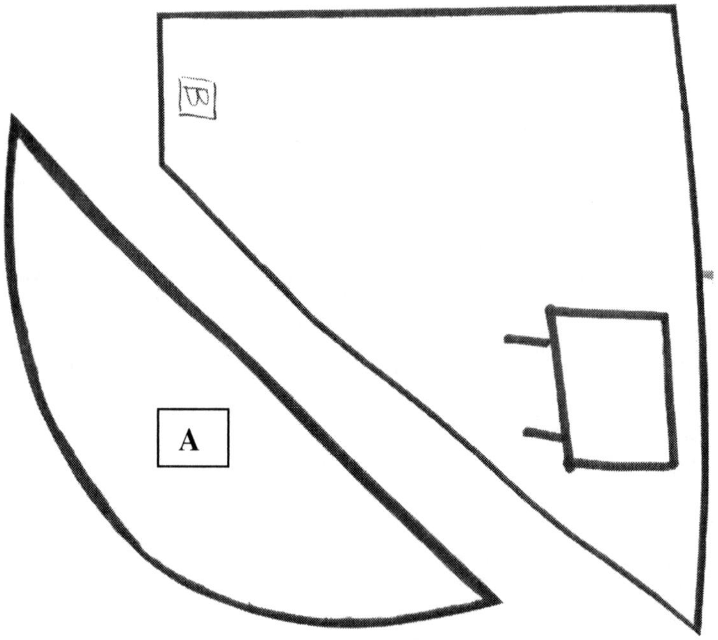

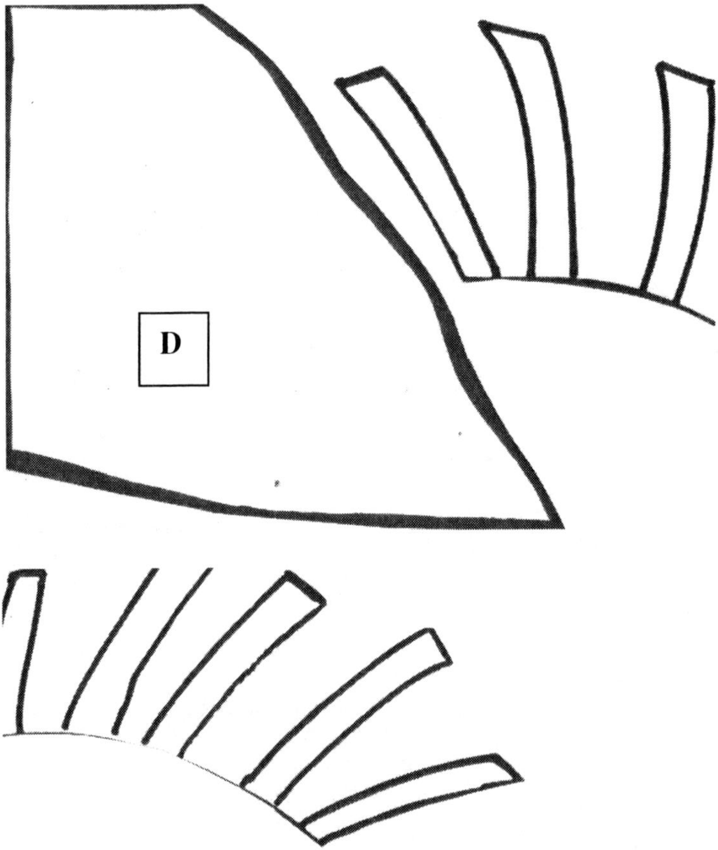
D

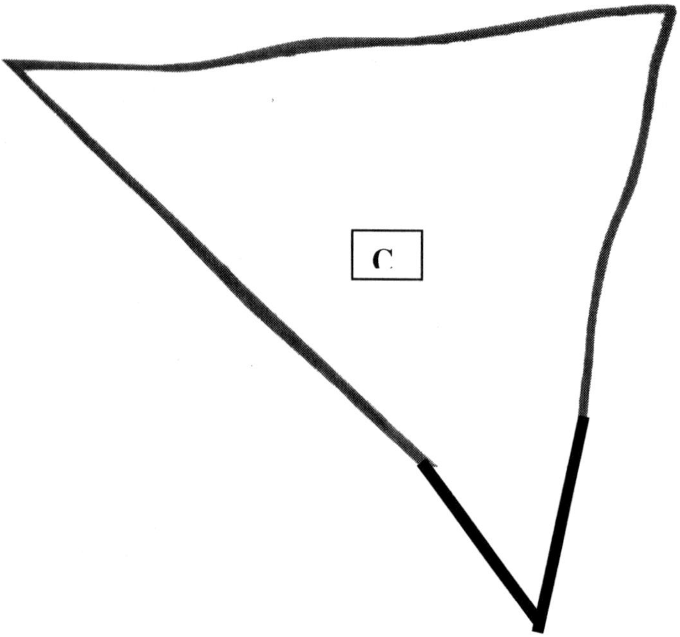
C

Appendix B
Quilting Resources

Quilting is enjoying a revival of sorts and there is an abundance of information available on the internet and in bookstores. Check with your local library as well. Listed below are a few resources to get you started if you think you're catching "Quilting Fever!"

Ehrlich, Laura *The Complete Idiot's Guide to Quilting*, 2nd Edition; Alpha: New York, 2004

"Quilting with a Passion!"
quiltingpassion.com/**resources**.html

"About Quilting"
quilting.about.com/library

Works Cited

Dobard, Raymond G. and Jacqueline L. Tobin *Hidden in Plain View: A Secret Story of Quilts and the Underground Railroad.* 2000

Gold, Taro, *Open Your Mind, Open Your Life.* Andrews Andrew McMeel Publishing: Kansas City, 2002

Gordon, Maggie McCormick, *The Quilter's Resource Book* Chrysalis: London 2004

Field, Reshad, *The Alchemy of the Heart.* Elements Books Limited: United Kingdom

Mountain Dreamer, Oriah, *The Invitation,* Harper Collins Publishing: New York, 1999

Myss, Carolyn, *Why People Don't Heal and How They Can,* Three Rivers Press, 1997

Siegel, Bernie, *Love, Medicine and Miracles*, Harper Perennial: New York, 1990

"A Collection of Notes on the Historical Aspects of Quilting" www.katerynedevelyn.org/quilting